WHY WAS JESUS BORN?

Written By: Laura M. Williams
Illustrated By: Barbara L. Finney

ISBN 9781628393460

www.xulonpress.com

WHY WAS JESUS BORN?

It wasn't to be the Son of Mary and Joseph,
for He is the Son of God.

It wasn't to be born in a palace,
for He was born in a stable.

It wasn't to have a beginning, for He is the
Alpha and Omega, the beginning and the end.

It wasn't to satisfy man's ideas,
but to complete His Father's perfect plan.

It wasn't to be
a prophet,
for He is
all knowing.

It wasn't to be
in the darkness,
for He brought Light
into this dark world.

WHY WAS JESUS BORN?

It wasn't for worldly power,
for all power is His.

It wasn't to be a carpenter, for He is
the Creator of the Universe.

It wasn't for fame and yet all
the world knows His name.

It wasn't for riches, for
He owns everything.

It wasn't to be a High Priest,
but your sacrifice.

It wasn't to sacrifice, but
to be the Perfect Sacrifice.

WHY WAS JESUS BORN?

It wasn't to be a Fisherman,
but a Fisher of men.

It wasn't to write or preach the Word,
He is the Word.

It wasn't to be a man,
for He is God.

It wasn't to pardon sin, but to
provide the only way of salvation.

It wasn't to be an earthly king,
for He is King of Kings.

It wasn't to provide a temporary kingdom,
for His kingdom lasts forever.

WHY WAS JESUS BORN?

It wasn't to make people love Him,
for many hated Him.

It wasn't to be defeated by death,
but to conquer death.

It wasn't to bring peace to a few,
for He is the Prince of Peace.

It wasn't to do His own thing,
but to obey His Father's will.

It wasn't to gain the trophies of this world, but to accomplish His Father's will.

It wasn't to condemn the world, but that He might lead sinners to repentance.

WHY WAS JESUS BORN?

JESUS WAS BORN TO DIE FOR YOU AND ME!

CPSIA information can be obtained at www.ICGtesting.com
Printed in the USA
LVOW02s0615120913

352115LV00005B/9/P